Quiet Moments
with
God

Published by Barbour Publishing, Inc., P.O. Box 719, Uhrichsville, Ohio 44683, www.barbourbooks.com

Our mission is to publish and distribute inspirational products offering exceptional value and biblical encouragement to the masses.

 Member of the
Evangelical Christian
Publishers Association

Printed in China.

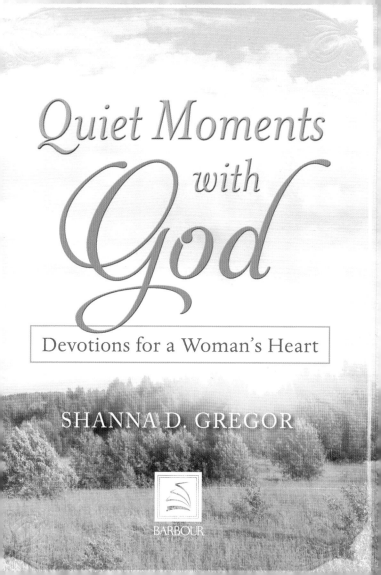

Quiet Moments with God

Devotions for a Woman's Heart

SHANNA D. GREGOR

BARBOUR

Contents

Imagine yourself sitting on your couch, comfortable and cozy, ready to spend some time visiting with your very best friend. *Quiet Moments with God* will inspire and encourage you to share your heart with a God who loves you. He has a purpose and a destiny awaiting you. As you grow closer to Him you'll discover just how much He loves you. He wants the very best for you. Time spent with Him will give Him the opportunity to speak to you each time you choose to come away with Him.

Battles are fought in our minds every day. When we begin to feel the battle is just too difficult and want to give up, we must choose to resist negative thoughts and be determined to rise above our problems. We must decide that we're not going to quit. When we're bombarded with doubts and fears, we must take a stand and say: "I'll never give up! God's on my side. He loves me, and He's helping me! I'm going to make it!"

JOYCE MEYER

Faith

Trust the Architect

Now faith is the substance
of things hoped for,
the evidence of things not seen.

HEBREWS 11:1 NKJV

If you've ever built a house from the ground up, you started with a blueprint. Unless you had a model to look at, you had only an idea of what the house would eventually look like when it was completed. The house was a work in progress—something not realized and not yet seen. As you watch the foundation being laid, the plumbing go in, and the walls go up, you can only imagine what it will look and feel like.

Building a home is a lot like living by faith. God, the Architect, has given you a blueprint of what it will look like found in the Bible. Through time spent with God in prayer, you come to know Him. You see the different pieces of your life coming together by His design.

Much like a contractor has challenges throughout the building stages, we face difficulties that challenge our faith. We have to trust that the blueprint is to the Architect's exact specifications. As you follow His lead, you will see His plan reflected in you.

Heavenly Father, sometimes I am tempted to doubt Your plans. I want to trust that You have every detail of my life ordered. Help me to lean into You and live by faith— knowing that You are the Master Architect with the perfect purpose for my life.

Faith and Action

So also faith by itself, if it does
not have works, is dead.

JAMES 2:17 ESV

❧

Heather and Cory purchased their first home with little money to spare. Unpacking the boxes, Heather tried not to look down. She didn't want to think about not having enough for new carpet. She had hoped the funds would come in. *After all,* she reasoned, *we have an infant who is starting to crawl and I don't want to have to keep him in the playpen all the time.*

Cory saw it on her face. "Okay," he said, "we're going to get new carpet!" Heather smiled, not sure what he meant. "We've been asking God for the money, but we need to do something." He pulled out a box knife and began cutting up the carpet and carrying the pieces to the garage. Heather was shocked but followed his lead and helped him get the carpet out of the house.

The next day Cory was assigned overtime in spite of cutbacks in other departments. A few weeks later, after reminding themselves daily that God would provide the money, there was enough money for the carpet. Heather realized that sometimes it took more than just telling God what you think you need—it can mean doing something while you're waiting.

Heavenly Father, when I have a need, show me what action I can take as I wait for You to provide for me.

A Reputation of Faith

But the path of the [uncompromisingly] just and righteous is like the light of dawn, that shines more and more (brighter and clearer) until [it reaches its full strength and glory in] the perfect day [to be prepared].

PROVERBS 4:18 AMP

Have you ever heard someone say, "His name is mud"? You might be surprised to find that it comes from the circumstances surrounding the assassination of President Abraham Lincoln in 1865. The reputation and life of Dr. Samuel A. Mudd was forever marred when he set the broken leg of John Wilkes Booth, Lincoln's assassin. Dr. Mudd went to prison because authorities felt he misled them by not reporting Booth's whereabouts. In 1869, President Andrew Johnson pardoned Dr. Mudd, but his reputation was lost to many.

Each day presents you with choices to demonstrate your relationship with God. It is in the quiet moments with God that you build your faith and find the strength to stand when your faith is tested. As others see you stand firm, they may be drawn to you as the Lord gives you an opportunity to share your faith with them.

God, help me to take time with You to build
my faith. Let my light shine as I grow in You—
during the difficult times and the times of peace—
so that my actions speak loudly for You!

Quiet Words of Strength and Life

Every part of Scripture is God-breathed and useful one way or another—showing us truth, exposing our rebellion, correcting our mistakes, training us to live God's way.

2 TIMOTHY 3:16 MSG

God breathed life into Adam, the first man. Just as oxygen is vital to life in the body—the Bible, God's Word, is vital to your spiritual survival. Quiet moments alone, drinking in the presence of God through His Word, are a feast of spiritual food to your spiritual self.

Sometimes you need answers that can only come within the truth of His Word. At other times your heart may become hard because you want to do things your own way. In those moments the scripture can shine light on your selfishness and give you the strength to choose to live your life God's way.

As you take time today, drink in His presence with each word. Slowly take in all that God wants to speak to you as you read His words of life and peace. Let them fill you with strength and assurance that He is more than enough.

Lord, help me to give Your Word first place in my life.
Open my heart to hear Your Truth and courage to
live my life the way You have commanded.

His Plans Are Better

He said to them, Because of the littleness of your
faith [that is, your lack of firmly relying trust]. For truly
I say to you, if you have faith [that is living] like a
grain of mustard seed, you can say to this mountain,
Move from here to yonder place, and it will move;
and nothing will be impossible to you.

MATTHEW 17:20 AMP

Graduation didn't hold the excitement and anticipation
Chandra had expected. Instead it hung like a dirty dishrag
of disappointment. All her efforts to find a job in the scope
of her degree seemed for nothing. Every small crack in
the door of opportunity was quickly slammed shut. Her
attempts to pray often ended in pity parties, whining to
God about what she wanted to do.

Her husband's ring tone on her phone startled her. Excited he said, "I've been offered a promotion. . .in Seattle." He paused, waiting for her reaction.

Her mind raced. The company headquarters where she worked part-time were located there. Her boss had suggested she apply for several of the openings in her field of study—but she knew her husband's job came first. "Oh honey—that's great!" she squealed. Peace flooded her heart. God's perfect timing would see her through again.

Lord, I have plans, but I know Your plans are better. Give me peace to wait on Your timing as I navigate by Your will instead of my own today.

Too Busy for God?

Come to me, all who labor and are heavy laden, and I will
give you rest. Take my yoke upon you, and learn from me,
for I am gentle and lowly in heart, and you will find rest for
your souls. For my yoke is easy, and my burden is light.
MATTHEW 11:28–30 ESV

Diana sat down in the classroom after first service, waiting
for Sunday school to start. Pat came in and sat next to her.
"You look a little distressed," Pat commented. "It's Pastor's
message," Diana replied. "'Are you too busy for God?' Just
yesterday I made a point to do much of nothing. Being
still is extremely difficult for me. I gave my body and mind
a rest. I watched two movies, puttered around the house,
and rested."

Pat smiled. "I think the point is that Satan loves for Christians to be too busy for God. When we do so much that we sacrifice our personal relationship with Him, then we lose focus. For me, that's when busyness is sin—when I'm doing something without Him. I've been guilty." Diana nodded in agreement.

Lord, I never want to be too busy to hear You. I need to hear from You every day. Your Word is a lamp for my feet and a light for my path. Without Your direction, I am tempted to take my own path. Help me to let go of the things that You don't want me to do today.

Nothing Short of a Miracle

But He said, "The things which are
impossible with men are possible with God."
LUKE 18:27 NKJV

✦

Hannah carried her second son full term. After a difficult pregnancy with her first son, delivering him five weeks early, she prayed for a healthy second pregnancy. She had experienced just that. But something had gone wrong.

After delivery, the baby had been taken to the neonatal intensive care unit with no hope for survival. The doctors discovered an unfamiliar bacterial infection. The baby was having difficulty breathing, and his blood count was deathly low. Hannah and her husband turned to God and were determined by faith for a miracle.

After four days with no assurance from the doctors that things would turn around, God made their faith a reality. "His blood counts are coming up," the doctor said, "and it wasn't really anything we did. Someone up there wanted this baby to live."

Hannah took her son for his six-week checkup. The doctor gave the baby a clean bill of health and said, "If I hadn't seen him in the hospital, I would not have believed he was the same baby. He's definitely nothing short of a miracle." Back in the car with the baby safely buckled into his car seat, tears came—tears of thankfulness that God still performs miracles today.

God, even when there is no hope
for what man can do, help me
to put my hope in You.

Only Believe

"He stood before me and said, 'Daniel, I have come to make things plain to you. You had no sooner started your prayer when the answer was given. And now I'm here to deliver the answer to you.'"

DANIEL 9:22 MSG

There are seasons in prayer when it seems that God has not heard your prayers. The more time passes, the more it feels like the answer will not come. Doubt tries to inch its way into your heart. Hold fast to your trust in God. He is faithful and hears the prayers of those who belong to Him.

Daniel fasted and prayed every day for an answer but heard nothing from heaven for three weeks (Daniel 10). Then God sent an angel named Gabriel to give Daniel the answer he so earnestly desired. It was not just an answer for Daniel, but an answer for his people—God's people.

When you hear the little voice of doubt encouraging you to give up, just believe. Hold fast to your faith, and press on harder. Spend more quiet time with God and listen. The answer will come in His time.

Lord, You know my heart and You know what I need before I even ask You. Give me the strength to wait on You and stand in faith for the answers I know will come.

Everlasting Love

The LORD has appeared of old to me, saying:
"Yes, I have loved you with an everlasting love;
therefore with lovingkindness I have drawn you."

JEREMIAH 31:3 NKJV

"Micah, you're really trying my patience," Belinda told her three-year-old. *Yeah, like he even knows what that means,* she thought to herself. He had refused to put his toys away, pulled all the laundry out of the hamper looking for his favorite red shirt that was dirty, and now he was refusing to sit at the table to eat his breakfast.

Belinda positioned her three-month-old daughter into her bouncy seat and snapped the straps in place. As she turned around she saw Micah carrying his cereal bowl overflowing with milk. "Micah, I told you. . ." But it was too late. Milk, cereal, and Micah flew into the air as he tripped over the baby's blankets on the floor.

Micah's face filled with fear as his eyes fell on his mother's face. Her face was red and she was about to blow her top. "Mommy! I'm sorry. . . ." He started to cry. Belinda held her breath as she tried to think of God as her own parent and the frustration He must sometimes feel with her. Her face relaxed and she pulled Micah into her lap and hugged him close.

Heavenly Father, thank You for Your everlasting love. Help me to remember as I try to please You that no matter how many times I fail, You love me unconditionally.

Time to Dream Again

We are pressed on every side by troubles,
but we are not crushed. We are perplexed,
but not driven to despair.

2 Corinthians 4:8 nlt

Turning thirty wasn't a highlight for Bridgett. The dreams she held for her life in her twenties were similar to her three-year-old daughter's ice cream cone that had melted into a sweet, sticky mess on the kitchen table, where she had left it.

As she cleaned up the gooey mess, she thought about how her plans were met with such resistance. She had gotten pregnant in college and classes had become too difficult, so she dropped out. With some flexibility in her schedule at the newspaper now, her husband had encouraged her to press through. "There's always going to be opposition to your dream. If school is right and you know it in your heart, you can do it!"

He was right. She had one more year to finish, and if she set her heart on this dream, God would help her. She needed to commit and stay strong to see it through. She logged on to the university website to begin taking action to press through to her dream.

Lord, there are dreams I have laid aside. It seemed like it was too hard. I ask You to reignite the fire and passion for the dreams You have put in my heart and give me the strength to pursue all You have for me.

Repentance removes old sins and
wrong attitudes, and it opens the way for
the Holy Spirit to restore our spiritual health.

SHIRLEY DOBSON

Forgiveness

Forgiveness Brings Restoration

For as the heavens are high above the earth, so great are His mercy and loving-kindness toward those who reverently and worshipfully fear Him. As far as the east is from the west, so far has He removed our transgressions from us.

PSALM 103:11–12 AMP

Adam and Eve walked with God. They talked with Him in the Garden He created for them (Genesis 3:8). Imagine the quiet, intimate moments they shared, discussing God's grand creation, their lives, and their future. Then something radically changed. With one decision, their whole world turned upside down. Adam and Eve's choice—their disobedience—immediately separated them from God. Instead of anticipating quiet walks and gentle conversations with their Father, they felt something they'd never known before—guilt and shame.

When they heard God in the Garden, their guilt compelled them to hide from Him. When they finally answered God they were held accountable for their choice—and suffered the consequences of their actions—but God in His mercy also forgave them.

Forgiveness brings restoration. Through salvation, God forgives and is always ready to help you through the circumstances of the sin you experienced, just as He helped Adam and Eve. Through His gift of salvation you can experience quiet moments walking with Him like Adam and Eve did long ago.

God, thank You for Your great mercy and love. Thank You that I am not alone, but that You are always there to be with me through every challenge I face—and every reason for celebration!

Run to God

"Come. Sit down. Let's argue this out." This is God's Message: "If your sins are blood-red, they'll be snow-white. If they're red like crimson, they'll be like wool."

ISAIAH 1:18 MSG

Leah was a mess. She found herself homeless, jobless, and hopeless. She sat on the steps of what *had been* her apartment. The rent hadn't been paid in months, and the landlord had changed the locks on the doors while she was out.

I'm thirty years old and I have nothing to show for my life, she thought. *I have nowhere to go—I've burned all my bridges.* She leaned back against the steps and her eyes wandered to a billboard above the building across the street. THERE'S STILL HOPE—RUN TO GOD, it read.

God seemed like Someone who lived ages ago. Then her heart leaped: *What if He is still here? What if He still cares? No one else can save me.* Emotion gushed within her—something she hadn't felt since she was a child. "God, is that You?" she prayed. "I don't want to waste any more of my life. Come into my heart and give me new life."

She stood up and slipped her backpack to her shoulder. She had to find a church and others who would help her know more about God.

Lord, forgive me for the times when I've tried to figure it all out on my own. Here I am today, running to You for the answers for my life.

A Brand-New Book

"Therefore I tell you, her sins, which are many, are forgiven—for she loved much. But he who is forgiven little, loves little." And he said to her, "Your sins are forgiven."

LUKE 7:47–48 ESV

Your life is a story. When you meet someone new, you may be quick to share your accomplishments, but are probably reluctant to share past failures or mistakes.

When you come to God and present Him with your life story, He takes that book of sins, mistakes, and failures that come from a life without Him and shreds each and every page. He forgives and forgets who you were without Him, and presents you with a clean, fresh book ready for a new story in Him.

Satan, your adversary, is quick to bring up the past. He wants to remind you of the old story, the book that can never be reprinted as it was. Through forgiveness and God's grace, you have a new life. Jesus paid the price and the enemy has no evidence of the past.

You don't have to ever go backward. If you make a mistake, He is quick to forgive and you are able to start again, new.

Heavenly Father, thank You for giving me a new life—a new book. Help me to write a story that brings You glory. Remind me that the debt is paid and I don't have to recount the past. I am a new book with a new story in You.

Open Hearts

*And be kind to one another, tenderhearted, forgiving
one another, even as God in Christ forgave you.*
EPHESIANS 4:32 NKJV

❧

Greg and Rachelle were in the kitchen cooking dinner
together while their daughter Maya worked on homework
at the bar. Greg noticed Maya had gotten a text and then
began to cry. He wiped his hands on a towel and walked
around to where his daughter was sitting. Concerned, he
asked, "What is it?"

Rachelle stopped what she was doing as Maya
explained about her friend Erica's situation. The two
girls had been close in middle school, but Erica had gone
to a different high school when her mother remarried.

Her stepbrother and stepfather were alcoholics and had become violent and abusive. When Erica had turned eighteen, the violence had escalated. She wanted to leave but had no place to go.

Greg looked at Rachelle and then asked, "Maya, is she someone you would bring into our home?" Maya nodded her head. "Well, meet her and bring her here for the weekend. We'll see where it goes from there."

A month later, Erica was still living with Maya's family. There had been some adjustment to the house rules, but Greg and Rachelle had offered her a home—for as long as she needed it.

Lord, show me how I can reach out to others.
Help me to recognize opportunities to demonstrate
Your love to others You bring across my path.

Doing It Right

"But when you are praying, first forgive anyone
you are holding a grudge against, so that your
Father in heaven will forgive your sins, too."

MARK 11:25 NLT

Carlie and Michael had a whirlwind relationship. They
were ready to settle down and get married. And when
Michael proposed just three months after their first date,
Carlie accepted. *He must be the one,* she thought. *He loves the*
Lord, and I think I could really be happy with him.

When they went to their pastor for premarital
counseling, he asked, "Do you know beyond a shadow of a
doubt that God destined the two of you to be married for
the rest of your lives?" Carlie wanted to say, "Yes!" but she

couldn't. She had doubts. She glanced quickly at Michael and could tell that he was also torn. A week later, Michael ended the relationship.

Carlie was hurt and embarrassed. Their relationship had been very public—and so had their breakup. Everyone knew. Resentment began to build. She went to the Lord and asked Him to help her forgive Michael and let go of the hurt. Once she did, she felt lighter and it got easier to be around him. Six months later she met Jason, and this time she knew they belonged together.

Lord, if there is someone I have not forgiven, or have hurt feelings toward, help me to lean on You and let go of that pain. Show me how to forgive and move forward.

Finding the True You

Make a clean break with all cutting, backbiting,
profane talk. Be gentle with one another, sensitive.
Forgive one another as quickly and thoroughly
as God in Christ forgave you.

Ephesians 4:31–32 msg

Cassie had been hurt by girlfriends in the past and refused
to give anyone another opportunity. Her smart remarks
and cutting words often sent people in the opposite
direction. Her heart was extremely guarded, even with
those who knew her best.

But something changed. She had gone to a Christian
retreat with a group of ladies at work. One of the ladies
gave her the trip as a gift. Cassie thought it was a great

opportunity to relax. The trip included time in the spa, massages, and an atmosphere of peace and tranquility. There were times when the group shared about their lives. Cassie saw something different and quietly asked God to be her friend.

She was slowly seeing God inside of her soften her heart. She was not so quick to judge others or snap at them. She began to open up and take counsel from these ladies. Through the Bible and her new relationship with God, she was finding she really liked the new person she was becoming.

Lord, create a new heart in me. Allow me to see myself as You see me. Show me what things I need to change to be more Christlike.

New Life

Then the Lord God formed man from the dust of the
ground and breathed into his nostrils the breath or
spirit of life, and man became a living being.

GENESIS 2:7 AMP

God created Adam from the dust of the earth. He formed
his body and then breathed life into his lungs. Today
dirt has little value—people don't think much of it. It's
unclean, impure, and sometimes contaminated. Yet, God
took dirt and made all of mankind.

This is a beautiful image of how God can take
something worthless and create a masterpiece. He can
take the things in our lives that bring us shame and hurt
and give them great value. Think of the things that you

perceive as ugly in your life: past mistakes, unspoken shames, words that scarred you, and grief that may still hurt today.

If you're willing to give it all to God, He can take those things and make something new. He can remove the pain and breathe new life into you. He can wash away the old hurts and fill you with His joy and strength. He can heal your hurts and bring you to a place where they become something new and beautiful in His eyes—and yours.

Lord, You know my past. You know my failures, hurts, and pains. I ask You today to heal me and make me whole. Breathe new life into me today and make me beautifully new—as only You can.

A Fresh Place to Start

*And He said to them, "Come aside by yourselves to a
deserted place and rest a while." For there were many
coming and going, and they did not even have time to eat.*

MARK 6:31 NKJV

Rushing from here to there, doing those things that must
be done. Life can get in the way of your relationships—
especially your relationship with God. Do you ever feel
guilty because you're "too busy for God"?

Jesus and His disciples were in ministry—working
for God and seeing to the needs of others. People were
constantly drawing from Jesus and His team to meet their
needs or answer their questions. There were times when

they just had too much going on. Jesus took time to rest, to get alone with God, to fellowship with Him and renew His spirit. He encouraged His disciples to do the same.

If you haven't been spending the time you know you need with the Father, take some time to hit the RESET button. Establish priorities and set time aside each day to get quiet with Him.

Father, forgive me for not making my time with You the top priority. Help me to start fresh today in keeping my commitment to feed my spirit during my quiet time with You.

Embrace Forgiveness

*Make allowance for each other's faults, and forgive
anyone who offends you. Remember, the Lord
forgave you, so you must forgive others.*

COLOSSIANS 3:13 NLT

God desires for you to live a healthy life. Throughout the
Bible, He commands you to forgive others. The choice to
forgive someone is often perceived as a gift given to the
one being forgiven, but in truth, the one who gives the gift
benefits the most.

The Mayo Clinic encourages patients to forgive in
order to experience healthier relationships and significant
spiritual and psychological well-being, and also to enjoy

less anxiety, stress, and hostility. They also list lower blood pressure and less symptoms of depression as benefits to choosing a lifestyle of forgiveness.

You can give a gift to others by letting go of those things you might be holding against them. It will prove to be a gift to yourself, as well. As you let go, you will find a new freedom in your heart and a closer relationship with God.

Lord, I want to live my life free of any bitterness or resentment. Give me the strength to let go of things I've been holding on to. Help me to forgive and truly live a life free of hurt and pain. I choose to embrace a life of forgiveness today.

Prayer is not monologue,
but dialogue. God's voice in response
to mine is its most essential part.
ANDREW MURRAY

Your Powerful Amen

When two of you get together on anything
at all on earth and make a prayer of it,
my Father in heaven goes into action.
MATTHEW 18:19 MSG

The worlds were created by the power of God's words:
"Let there be light. . . . Let there be an expanse. . .let it
separate the waters. . . . Let the earth sprout vegetation"
(Genesis 1:3, 6, 11 ESV). God spoke the word and whatever
He declared came to be. Because man is created in the
image of God and has been given authority on the earth,
what people say matters. There is great power in the
spoken word.

The word *amen* has been spoken for hundreds of generations, usually at the close of a prayer. The word has great power and meaning behind it. *Amen* literally lends agreement among those who say it. It means "let it be established" or "let it be so."

Amen provides power by placing your agreement behind whatever has been said. It reinforces the prayers that have been prayed or the declarations that have been made. Take care to recognize what you are agreeing with when you say, "Amen."

Father, thank You for giving me power and authority through my relationship with You. I don't want to be frivolous with my words, but lend agreement to what You have said about my life, my family, and my world. Help me to be a good steward of the words I speak and the power in each Amen!

Passing the Blessing

Know therefore that the Lord your God is God,
the faithful God who keeps covenant and steadfast
love with those who love him and keep his
commandments, to a thousand generations.

DEUTERONOMY 7:9 ESV

Kendra's memories of her grandmother were full of times of prayer. She woke early in the morning and her soft, gentle voice could be heard down the hall into the guest room where Kendra and her cousin slept. She recalled how Grandma's voice would rise with authority as she prayed for healing for her when she was sick or hurt; and she would speak blessings of favor over them as they traveled home. Although Grandma went to heaven while Kendra was in college, she knew Grandma's prayers were still in God's heart.

Now as the mother of adult children, Kendra reflected on her grandmother's prayers in her children's lives. When Kendra prayed for them, she remembered the prayers of protection, blessing, and favor her grandmother prayed for her and all their future generations. She believed her own prayers, joined with generations before, would bring God's blessing into their family for generations to come.

Heavenly Father, thank You for the prayers of those who prayed for me. Help me to be mindful that prayers don't end with me, but can carry into future generations. Remind me to pray and bless those I may never meet in this life.

Helping Hands

*I have written to you who are God's children because you
know the Father. I have written to you who are mature in
the faith because you know Christ, who existed from the
beginning. I have written to you who are young in the faith
because you are strong. God's word lives in your hearts,
and you have won your battle with the evil one.*

1 JOHN 2:14 NLT

Devastating fires burned more than two hundred homes in
their small community. As Regina and Paul returned to the
place they called home for more than twenty years, there
were no tears. Regina could hardly breathe. She watched
her husband poke at the still-smoldering ashes with the
end of his shovel.

Everything was gone. Then she realized many from her church family had arrived. Quietly, they gathered around the couple and began to take one another's hands. Their pastor's words were just what she needed to hear. "Paul and Regina, you are not alone. We love you, support you, and will be here for you. We agree with you for God to provide everything you need." With each comforting hug, she began to breathe more. God would restore. It wouldn't be easy, she knew, but knowing there were many helping hands gave her hope.

Lord, thank You for my church family and friends. Help me to lean on them when I need support, and show me how I can help others in their time of need.

The Father Is Listening

*Give ear to my words, O L*ORD*, consider my meditation.*
Give heed to the voice of my cry, my King and my God,
for to You I will pray. My voice You shall hear in the
*morning, O L*ORD*; in the morning I will direct*
it to You, and I will look up.

PSALM 5:1–3 NKJV

Jasmine's heart had been broken after her parents' divorce.
After living her first twelve years in the same town, going
to the same school, and growing up with the same group
of friends, her mother had taken her away from everything
she'd ever known. After several months, her father had
stopped all contact—no phone calls, no birthday cards or
Christmas presents in the last year.

After a difficult day at school, she knocked on her mom's bedroom door. "Not now," her mom cooed. Jasmine knew she was on the phone with her boyfriend. This new relationship had cut deep into her once close relationship with her mom.

She walked slowly down the hall lost in her thoughts. *I was there for Mom when she had no one. No one is here, now, for me.* She closed her bedroom door and the tears came. Deep in her heart as the sobbing subsided, she heard the Lord speak. *"Jasmine, I'm here. I never left. . .and I am listening."*

Lord, help me to remember that I am never alone. I can always call on You and know that no matter what I am going through, You are with me, listening.

The Revelation of the Truth

He said to them, But who do you [yourselves] say that I am? Simon Peter replied, You are the Christ, the Son of the living God. Then Jesus answered him, Blessed (happy, fortunate, and to be envied) are you, Simon Bar-Jonah. For flesh and blood [men] have not revealed this to you, but My Father Who is in heaven.

MATTHEW 16:15–17 AMP

Tanya struggled to understand her father's resistance to God, especially after the miraculous work He had done in Tanya's life. She shared her faith, rather loudly at first. She fought with all her strength—at times—to make him understand.

"A belief in God is for those who are weak, who need something to believe in just to get through life," he had told her. As the years passed, he scoffed at her beliefs.

Tanya shared her struggle with her friend Rachel. Gently Rachel replied, "It's not a gift you can make your dad understand. His heart must open up to the truth of God's love."

Immediately Tanya stopped pushing her father toward God and began to trust God to speak to his heart. When her father was ready, Tanya would be there to answer his questions.

Lord, I have loved ones who need to know You. Lead me in my prayers for them and open their hearts to hear the truth of Your love. Show me how to be ready to help them when they do come to know You as I do.

God's Smile

Who would think of setting up pagan idols in God's holy Temple? But that is exactly what we are, each of us a temple in whom God lives. God himself put it this way: "I'll live in them, move into them; I'll be their God and they'll be my people."

2 CORINTHIANS 6:16 MSG

❧❧❧

Sarah looked at her brother, Hank. Something was different from the last time she'd seen him. It was something deeper than a different haircut or the fact that he'd shaved his beard. It wasn't a change in weight, either—although he did look a little thinner. It was a different attitude—a glow about him that seemed to come from his heart.

"Okay, spill," she said. "What's different?" Hank smiled. "Glad you noticed. I thought you might. It's not anything physical," he admitted. "It's a difference on the inside. I found Christ and now He lives in me. My heart is clean—Jesus has made me new."

Sarah looked away for a minute. She had prayed for a long time for her brother to come to know the Lord. She blinked back her tears and said, "It's as if the very smile of God has rested deep within your heart. His reflection is shining out for all to see." Then she put her arms around her brother and hugged him tight.

Lord, thank You for Your peace flowing in my heart.
May Your presence be reflected from my soul for all to see.

Hold On to the Truth

See to it that no one takes you captive by philosophy and empty deceit, according to human tradition, according to the elemental spirits of the world, and not according to Christ.

COLOSSIANS 2:8 ESV

Sonya stood in line waiting to pay for the last of her books for her third semester in college. She had avoided the humanities classes required for her degree as long as she could. She had heard horror stories from classmates who came out of their sociology and psychology classes completely confused and not sure what they believed when it came to their faith. She was determined to hold on to the truth as she endured these classes.

She felt she knew the Word, she knew who she was in her relationship with Christ, but she wanted to be ready to withstand the challenge. She was determined to take the information given to her by her professors and classmates and hold it up to the light of the Word of God. Each assignment, each contradiction to the Word of God, was a difficult fight, but at the end of the semester she had grown in her understanding of her faith and in her relationship with God.

Heavenly Father, teach me Your Word. Give me revelation, insight, and understanding as I read Your words for my life each day. Help me to hold on to the truth as I come to know You even more.

You Can Hear God

Then Mary said, "Behold the maidservant of
the Lord! Let it be to me according to your word."
And the angel departed from her.

LUKE 1:38 NKJV

❧

God's Word is very specific about what is right and wrong, but it doesn't always give you specifics like whom to marry, what job to take, or when to make big decisions in your life. The Bible says there is wisdom in the counsel of many, and there are times when it's good to have the input of others. But it's also very important to hear from God for yourself.

Mary was engaged to a man named Joseph, and yet the angel of the Lord told her she would have God's child without knowing a man. Imagine what could have run through her mind—Joseph could refuse to marry her and think she'd been unfaithful. Yet she accepted God's plan and trusted Him to work out the details.

Others may have voiced their concern to Joseph and suggested he not go through with the wedding, but God assured Joseph that Mary was telling him the truth. Others might have not agreed with Mary and Joseph's plans, but they each knew they had heard the voice of God and agreed to do what God asked of them.

God, forgive me for asking everyone else what they think, instead of coming to You first with my choices. Help me to know Your voice and agree with Your Word today.

It's the Truth You Know

Accept other believers who are weak in faith, and don't argue with them about what they think is right or wrong.

ROMANS 14:1 NLT

✦

Some people love a good debate. The problem is, winning the debate can be more important than building relationships with others. Friendships dissolve, marriages are destroyed, and family ties are strained at every family gathering because someone values his or her own opinion more than the hearts of loved ones.

Even Christians today wage wars between denominations and even within their own church families over what they believe the Bible to mean. That is not God's desire. He commands us to love one another.

Demonstrating that love means gently sharing your beliefs, but allowing others room to explore their faith and "work out their own salvation."

The most important relationship anyone has is their relationship with God. He searches their hearts and reveals the truth. When you meet someone who is very opinionated or offers up debate, respond with love and grace. Share your wisdom peacefully, and if they resist, bow out. Give them space to grow and pray for them.

Father, teach me Your truths and show me how to share those truths in love with others. Give me wisdom and discernment so that I know when to share, and when to hold things in my heart. Help me to respond in love and trust that You will show them the right path.

God's Word in the Mirror

And let your instruction be sound and fit and wise and wholesome, vigorous and irrefutable and above censure, so that the opponent may be put to shame, finding nothing discrediting or evil to say about us.

TITUS 2:8 AMP

The Bible, God's Word, demonstrates who God is and what He does. His Word is His nature, character, and integrity. If God said it, you can believe it. When you put His Word in your heart and make it a part of who you are, you connect your faith with His and amazing things can happen.

Speaking His Word to Him in prayer is like holding a mirror in front of Him. Your words and your life reflect His image and His promises. As you agree with His truth, you become more like Him. As you choose to do life His way, your choices for life align to His will. His purpose and plan begin to grow in you, fulfilling all the potential He put in you. Believe in your heart His promises are truly for you.

Heavenly Father, teach me Your Word. Prepare my heart as I lay it open to receive Your instruction. Help me to become more like You, reflecting Your image each day.

Women need real moments of solitude
and self-reflection to balance out how
much of ourselves we give away.
DR. BARBARA DE ANGELIS

Dedication

Mistaken for Christ

*God wanted everyone, not just Jews, to know this rich
and glorious secret inside and out, regardless of their
background, regardless of their religious standing. The
mystery in a nutshell is just this: Christ is in you, so
therefore you can look forward to sharing in God's glory.
It's that simple. That is the substance of our Message.*

COLOSSIANS 1:27 MSG

Have you ever been mistaken for someone other than
yourself? Perhaps someone waved at you from across the
parking lot and called you by a name other than your own.
They were mistaken about your identity. You may have
looked familiar to them or had similar characteristics that
made them believe—even just for a second—that you were
someone they knew.

Jesus Christ came to teach all people how to live a life pleasing to the heavenly Father. He came to live an example of how everyone can know the Father through Him. He constantly, even today, points others to God. Believers are encouraged to imitate Christ. Paul said, "Imitate me, just as I imitate Christ" (1 Corinthians 11:1 NLT). He followed Jesus' example and led others to know Him and to know the Father.

So, are you living your life in a way today that you could be mistaken for Christ?

Jesus, thank You for Your example. I want to look like You. I want to follow Your example and become the image of Your character and nature. I want to reflect You in such a way that others see You instead of me.

Call His Name

And I tell you, ask, and it will be given to you; seek,
and you will find; knock, and it will be opened to you.
For everyone who asks receives, and the one who seeks
finds, and to the one who knocks it will be opened.

LUKE 11:9–10 ESV

❧

Have you ever been lost? Perhaps you were separated from your mother in a department store as a child, or you took a wrong turn and weren't sure how you would get back to a familiar place. It can be frightening when you are separated from those you love or can't find your way.

Your heavenly Father has promised to never leave you or forsake you. He is with you at all times. When you feel lost or alone, all you have to do is call on Him. When you speak His name, He is there, ready to assure you and calm your fears. It is never so dark that He can't find you or so chaotic that He won't hear you. Rest assured that when you call on Him, He'll be there for you.

Heavenly Father, I don't want to wait until I feel lost and alone before I call on You. Help me to cherish my time with You, enjoying Your presence and getting to know You more each day.

Treasured Relationship

For where your treasure is,
there your heart will be also.
Luke 12:34 NKJV

God gave His best gift—His only Son—in hope of a relationship with His creation. He applied His faith believing that as He sacrificed Jesus, all men would have the opportunity to know Him, accept Him, and spend eternity with Him. Jesus was His only Son, and yet He was willing to pour out His blood to open the way for you to come to Him.

He put His money where His mouth was—so to speak. He gave His Son with a great expectation of having many sons and daughters. The earth is the Lord's and everything within it. He lacks no good thing and has no need of any of it. He does not place value on the things in this earth—gold, silver, diamonds, and wealth that men seek. His treasure—what He esteems as the greatest value—is a relationship with each and every person He created. You are His treasure. He willingly sacrificed it all, trusting you would come to know Him and love Him.

Father, thank You for creating me and calling me Your own. I am honored to know that You prize me above all other things in the earth. I am Your treasure. Help me to see myself as You do today.

Waiting with God

Lord, where do I put my hope?
My only hope is in you.
PSALM 39:7 NLT

❧

No one enjoys waiting. Whether it's the long lines at the grocery stores, a stack of cars at a red light, or waiting for the doors to open at a concert, it's perceived as a delay or a moment in time when nothing is happening.

The truth is, when it comes to a relationship with God, waiting doesn't mean there is no forward progression. God is always at work behind the scenes doing what He does best to bring out His promises for your life. You can't always see the work He is doing. It can be challenging to pray and believe when there is no physical evidence that your dreams are becoming a reality, but He is your hope.

When you wait on God, you can take action each day by speaking to Him about the things He has promised you. You can remain positive instead of critical. Put His promises in your mouth and keep them flowing through your heart and mind. He will do what He has promised.

Lord, I am waiting and trusting. I am not sitting idle, but I am applying my faith and believing that You will deliver on Your promises. It may not look like I think it will, but I know You are bringing Your very best into my life. I trust You.

Higher Expectations

Be strong and let your heart take courage,
all you who wait for and hope for and expect the Lord!
PSALM 31:24 AMP

❦

We all know at least one worrywart—someone who just can't resist fretting about "what if." Worrying opens the door for fear to creep into our minds and block our view of God's faithfulness, but the psalmist tells us to be of good courage. As a result of his own experiences with the goodness of God and of His gracious protection in times of danger, he exhorts us to be encouraged, and to feel assured that God will not leave or forsake us.

When we put our hope in the Lord, He strengthens our hearts—He animates us and enables us to meet trials and opposition. He keeps us from becoming faint and disheartened.

God alone can give us success. If our hope centers on the Lord, then we are not relying on the fleeting things of this world or our own strength to sustain us. Our heavenly Father makes our lives happy and prosperous. He provides for our needs, cheers us, and comforts us. Even death, through Him, is serene and triumphant as we know that heaven awaits.

Heavenly Father, sometimes I think that I have to do things on my own. I allow worry and fear to rule in my life, and I forget that You are always faithful to Your children. Help me to remember that my hope and strength is in You, Lord.

Devoted to You

May GOD, our very own God, continue to be with
us just as he was with our ancestors—may he never give
up and walk out on us. May he keep us centered and
devoted to him, following the life path he has cleared,
watching the signposts, walking at the pace and
rhythms he laid down for our ancestors.

1 KINGS 8:57–58 MSG

Hannah had trust issues. Her father walked out when she was a tween. The few times she had reconnected with him led to disappointment. So, the illustration of God being a trustworthy, loving Father had more of a negative impact on Hannah than a positive one. Her memories of her father brought up disappointment, hurt, guilt, shame, and resentment.

But something was different. There was a presence and a peace like she'd never known that drew her in, that caused her to search Him out, ask questions in her heart, and study the Bible. She wanted to know Him; she needed to know what a father should have been.

Very slowly, and gently, she opened the door and let Him in. He began to demonstrate His faithfulness in her life, and she discovered Him to be devoted to her like no one had ever been in her life.

Father, I want to know You more.
Thank You for Your unfailing faithfulness
and never-ending love. Draw me closer to
You and teach me to trust You more each day.

Remember Me?

Whoever trusts in his riches will fall,
but the righteous will flourish like a green leaf.
PROVERBS 11:28 ESV

❦

LeAnn was picking up some things at her local grocery store when she unexpectedly found herself in line behind Ted Danson. She smiled and blurted out, "Good to see you—I loved *Cheers!*" He mumbled, "Thanks," and ran to his car. Embarrassed by her fan-crazed, paparazzi-style approach to introducing herself, she, too, quietly exited the store and disappeared into her car. Driving home she felt a little guilty because she had blurted out to him that she remembered him for a television show he starred in more than twenty years ago, instead of the hit drama he currently starred in every week.

Individually each person is known for different things on the earth. What do people remember about you? It's not the Hollywood superstars who make the biggest impact in the lives of those around you—but the little day-to-day choices you make in your personal life that can bring a big influence in the lives of those you touch each day.

Lord, I love You. I want the light of Your goodness to shine through my life in all I do. Remind me to let the little choices I make speak volumes to those around me. Help me hold fast to Your life-giving truths and offer a legacy that leads others directly to You.

Love's Language

But let all those rejoice who put their trust in You;
let them ever shout for joy, because You defend them;
let those also who love Your name be joyful in You.
For You, O Lord, will bless the righteous; with
favor You will surround him as with a shield.

PSALM 5:11–12 NKJV

Jana had waited years to volunteer in the neonatal
intensive care unit at the local hospital. Her own daughter
had received excellent treatment there almost twenty years
before. She listened intently as the trainer explained how
premature babies speak their own language, signaling to
caregivers if they are comfortable or stressed-out.

Likewise, love is a language of its own. As you communicate love to others, it resets the temperatures of the relationships you have. Love chooses to put the needs of others before your own. It embraces rather than repels and comforts with a heavenly compassion. It says, "Yes you can!" Love is a positive force that elevates those around you and brings them closer to the heart of God.

God, I want to speak the language of love. Remind me to pause and take a breath so I can see others as You see them. Help me take my eyes off of me and really take the time to speak love's language to everyone around me.

God, Be the Boss of Me

Protect me, for I am devoted to you. Save me,
for I serve you and trust you. You are my God.
PSALM 86:2 NLT

❧

If you've been in a house full of kids, you've most likely heard one telling the other one what to do. Sometimes it escalates to the point that someone says, "You're not the boss of me!" Maybe you remember saying that to someone yourself when you were a child.

When you invited Jesus into your heart, to be the Lord of your life—you gave Him the right to be the boss of your life. If you've been baptized, you made a public profession of your faith, declaring His lordship over your life. Imagine yourself coming up out of that water declaring boldly, "God, be the boss of me!"

He wants you to give Him everything—every decision—every concern. When you're struggling with something, remember, you gave your life to Him. He's the leader for you to follow. Let go of the worry and turn the situation over to Him. He's ready to show you His ways.

God, be the boss of me! I lean on Your understanding
and accept Your ways. I will do my life Your way.
All that I am struggling with—I release it into
Your care, and I wait for Your direction.
Show me the way today.

It does not take great men to do great things;
it only takes consecrated men.
PHILLIPS BROOKS

Inspire Them to Ask

Then you will seek Me, inquire for, and require Me
[as a vital necessity] and find Me when you
search for Me with all your heart.

JEREMIAH 29:13 AMP

❧

Michael's job kept him away from the family more than he or Ella liked. She found herself doing more and more on her own. She worked to keep a joyful heart in the midst of this season in their lives. "Someday," she told herself, "it won't be this way."

She pushed her grocery cart up and down the aisle with a toddler in the seat and her five-year-old "helping" her get the things she needed. She noticed another lady watching her who spoke up, "You have such patience with your son and such a joyful attitude in the midst of all these grouchy grocery shoppers. How do you do it?"

Ella smiled at the lady and said softly, "It's not easy, but my joy comes from spending time each day with the Lord." Ella had learned that her job as a believer wasn't proclaiming the answer but inspiring the world to ask the question.

Heavenly Father, I want to be full of Your joy.
As I take time with You, fill me up with Your joy
so that others are inspired to ask about You.

See What He Sees

But the LORD said to Samuel, "Do not look at his appearance or at his physical stature, because I have refused him. For the LORD does not see as man sees; for man looks at the outward appearance, but the LORD looks at the heart."

1 SAMUEL 16:7 NKJV

※

Bridgette's heart ached. First she asked what she had done wrong as a parent. She raised her daughter with the help of the Lord and taught her right and wrong. Now, nearly fifteen years old, Brooklyn favored pleasing her friends over obeying her parents.

As a mother of a strong-willed daughter, Bridgette chose her battles carefully and prayed constantly. Daily she spent time on her knees, concerned about the choices her daughter was making and the behavior she was displaying.

One morning as she studied the Bible and talked to God, a great peace settled over her. She read the scripture in 1 Samuel 16 and felt the Lord's assurance that He saw something differently in Brooklyn.

She was determined to change gears. Instead of telling the Lord all the things about her daughter that He already knew, she decided to begin to thank Him for the daughter she would become—the daughter He sees.

Lord, help me to see others through Your eyes.
When I feel like people are not responding
the way a Christian should, help me to
love them with Your perspective.

Draw the Line on God's Side

By faith, Noah built a ship in the middle of dry land.
He was warned about something he couldn't see, and acted
on what he was told. The result? His family was saved.
His act of faith drew a sharp line between the evil of the
unbelieving world and the rightness of the believing world.
As a result, Noah became intimate with God.

HEBREWS 11:7 MSG

With news and information at your fingertips, it can keep you focused on the world. God desires for you to live focused on His vision for your life. When you choose His ways, you align yourself with God instead of today's culture.

Noah was aware of the lifestyle choices people made, but he was not fixed on them. He was determined to align himself with God's direction and grow in relationship with God.

Noah's choices to do things God's way set him apart from others. His neighbors found him very strange—a man building a giant boat in a world that had never seen rain. Noah faithfully invited others to know God and join his pending adventure. He trusted God for the boat to eventually float. He drew a line in the sand on God's side of truth and saved his own life and the lives of his family.

Lord, help me to live my life on Your side of the line.
I want others to see such a difference in me
that it opens their hearts to know You.

Set Apart for a Purpose

Do not be conformed to this world, but be transformed
by the renewal of your mind, that by testing you
may discern what is the will of God, what is
good and acceptable and perfect.

ROMANS 12:2 ESV

Jesus didn't live His life secluded from the world. He was in the world, but not of the world. He lived each day consecrated to God. He fed His spirit man with the Word of God and time with God in prayer so that He could live God's way within the world.

The more you know the Word of God, the more you understand God and His ways. You come to know God's character and nature—what pleases Him and what disappoints Him. You discover how He operates within the world, as well as the authority and dominion He's given you as His child.

You have been chosen and set apart for God's purpose. When you take the time to know Him, you will discover the life He has chosen for you—fulfilling the will of God just as Jesus did.

Father, I want to live my life consecrated to You.
Remind me how important it is to know You. Help
me to set my priorities correctly, putting my time
with You in prayer and in the Word first.

With Your Whole Heart

With my whole heart I have sought You;
oh, let me not wander from Your commandments!
PSALM 119:10 NKJV

The psalmist says he sought God with his whole heart. When you put your whole heart to something, you're committed. You're holding fast—refusing to give up. You spend every waking moment thinking about it, talking about it, consumed by it.

When a young couple dreams of starting a family and has a desire to get pregnant, it consumes them. When someone is looking for that first new house, it's what they think about and dream about. When you meet someone who may become your future spouse, you pursue them.

You give your whole heart to that dream—that possibility of having a baby, owning a home, or spending the rest of your life with someone.

That same passion, energy, and pursuit is exactly the experience the psalmist is describing. Your relationship with God can be a deep pursuit. In your quiet time, pursue Him. Open your heart, speak to Him, and let His presence consume you.

Heavenly Father, I open my heart to You. Consume me with Your presence and meet me in my quiet time as I grow to know You more intimately.

Rescued

But you are not like that, for you are a chosen people. You are royal priests, a holy nation, God's very own possession. As a result, you can show others the goodness of God, for he called you out of the darkness into his wonderful light.

1 PETER 2:9 NLT

❧

Paula and her husband, Kurt, had a stray cat that would hide her kittens each year in the strangest places on their property. One spring Paula discovered four tiny kittens up a tree. A few evenings later the kittens became stranded during a storm expected to turn violent.

Paula convinced Kurt to help her save them. She stood with an umbrella and raincoat, holding a flashlight until Kurt got them all safely out of the tree and into a laundry basket full of towels. Inside the house, she checked each one to make sure they were okay.

When the mother never returned, Kurt built a little place for the kittens on the front porch to stay until they found homes for them. One afternoon while they were waiting for a family to arrive to adopt the last little kitten, Kurt looked at Paula. "You rescued those kittens," he said, "like God rescued me. When I thought no one cared, and I had nothing left to live for, God came in and said He wanted me."

Father, thank You for rescuing me. You were there when I felt alone and thought no one cared. I want to live each day for You.

Like Father, Like Daughter

As in water face reflects face,
so a man's heart reveals the man.
PROVERBS 27:19 NKJV

✦

Family resemblances are sometimes undeniable. Perhaps you've seen a daughter who is the spitting image of her mother, or a son who could win a "mini-me" contest when paired with his father. It seems there is often something familiar that connects family members, and others outside the family almost instantly know they belong together. Sometimes there is no biological connection, such as the case of adoption or stepfamilies, and yet people continue to point out a family resemblance they see.

God often does that to show you that you may not have grown up physically knowing Him, but spiritually, once you become His child, there is a strong family resemblance. As you grow in your relationship with Him, you begin to "look" like Him. Your words begin to align with His Word. Your choices and decisions in life begin to reflect His will and desire for your life.

You were created to demonstrate your heavenly Father's image in all that you do and say. Do you see a strong family resemblance to your heavenly Father? Do others see Him in you?

Father, I want to please You. I want others to see You in me. Fill me with Your presence today. Lead me, guide me, correct me, and show me Your ways that I may grow each day to be more and more like You.

Know Your Lines

Christ's life showed me how, and enabled me to do it.
I identified myself completely with him. Indeed, I have
been crucified with Christ. My ego is no longer central.
It is no longer important that I appear righteous before
you or have your good opinion, and I am no longer driven
to impress God. Christ lives in me. The life you see me
living is not "mine," but it is lived by faith in the Son of
God, who loved me and gave himself for me.

GALATIANS 2:20 MSG

"All the world's a stage" opens a monologue from William Shakespeare's play *As You Like It*. If everyone is a player on life's stage, then it is important to know your lines. The Word of God has answers for every situation in life.

"Jesus said to them, 'Truly, truly, I say to you, the Son can do nothing of his own accord, but only what he sees the Father doing. For whatever the Father does, that the Son does likewise'" (John 5:19 ESV).

As you study God's Word, you will discover God's way of doing things. As you put His ways into practice into every area of your life, you'll discover how He intended for you to live your life. You have the answers in His Word. Take time today to learn your lines.

Father, I desire to know Your Word. As I study, help me to hide Your Word in my heart so that I will respond to life as You would have me respond.

God at Work

For we are his workmanship, created in Christ Jesus
for good works, which God prepared beforehand,
that we should walk in them.

Ephesians 2:10 esv

As an artist begins creating a masterpiece, she has a
vision, a purpose, and a plan. As she begins to work she
is creating, imagining the outcome of her design. It will
become something extraordinary, something beautiful,
something good. It will delight her heart and bring joy
and goodness into the lives of others. It will be useful, and
serve a specific purpose that only she knows about as she
puts the pieces together.

Before you ever lived a day, God imagined you. He
knew you in His heart and mind before you ever came to

be. He believed you to be extraordinary, beautiful, and good. He designed you for His pleasure—to see you serve Him in a specific way. He filled you with talent and gifts that only you possess. He placed you into relationships in the lives of others that only you can touch.

You are God's work! He has created you as His own masterpiece and given you everything you need to become the exquisite, unique part of eternity.

Heavenly Father, show me the gifts and talents You have placed in me. Give me direction in how I am to fulfill Your purpose for my life. I am a willing work, molded by Your hand. Teach me more about my part in Your perfect plan.

Living with Margin to Spare

*As You sent Me into the world, I also have sent them
into the world. And for their sakes I sanctify Myself,
that they also may be sanctified by the truth.*

JOHN 17:18–19 NKJV

Gretchen's mother, Gwen, loved books. She had grown
up with a house full of them. It was uncommon to walk
through the house without finding a book in each room
laid open to the place where her mom was currently
reading. Gretchen shared her mother's passion, but her
busy life seldom gave her opportunity to feed that passion.

One cold, dreary afternoon Gretchen reached for a
book, an old favorite that she had read many times before.

It was worn and the pages were frayed. As she flipped through it to find a particular passage she was searching for she stopped. She realized most of the margins were all filled in with her notes. There wasn't a single place for more ink on most of the pages.

She sighed thinking to herself, *This is the way my life is. I am so busy with so many things I have no margin—no white space to breathe.*

Lord, help me to set my priorities according to Your desires and plans for my life. Show me how to live each day balanced with plenty of margin to spare.

The reason why many fail in battle is because they wait until the hour of battle. The reason why others succeed is because they have gained their victory on their knees long before the battle came. . . . Anticipate your battles; fight them on your knees before temptation comes, and you will always have victory.

REUBEN ARCHER TORREY

Your Ultimate Purpose

You who love the Lord, hate evil!
He preserves the souls of His saints;
He delivers them out of the hand of the wicked.

PSALM 97:10 NKJV

❧

Trena watched as her daughter, Amanda, let the front door slam behind her. She could immediately tell it had not been a good day at school. "Do you want to talk about it?" she asked.

"I just don't know why God created people," Amanda snapped. "The world is so upside down and completely opposite of what God wants for our lives. People are just evil. They take advantage of others, only look out for themselves, and will use anyone and anything to get what they want. And that is just high school!"

"Oh honey, I'm sorry it's so tough. You've got to remember that for the most part, these people have no desire in life to please God. If you love the Lord, you come to despise evil. We are not like the world. As believers, our ultimate purpose is to please God. The more we desire to please Him, the more our own desires line up with God's desires." Trena smiled.

"So, why are you smiling?" Amanda asked.

"I am proud of you. You are growing in the Lord. You are learning to love God's ways and hate the ways of the world—even the socially acceptable ones."

*Heavenly Father, teach me Your ways
so that my own desires line up with Yours!*

God's Peace

Don't worry about anything; instead, pray about everything. Tell God what you need, and thank him for all he has done. Then you will experience God's peace, which exceeds anything we can understand. His peace will guard your hearts and minds as you live in Christ Jesus.

PHILIPPIANS 4:6–7 NLT

Vivian lay in bed, wide awake and jealous of her husband snoring next to her. He fell asleep the minute his head hit the pillow, but she had to work hard to get her mind to wind down. She replayed the events of the day and thought about tasks she needed to do the next day. She worried she might have said things too harshly to a coworker. She regretted not taking a moment to encourage a friend.

She slipped out from her covers and grabbed her notebook. "God, You didn't create me to worry. Your Bible tells me to rest and rely on You," she prayed. She wrote down all the concerns running around in her head. Then she prayed, purposefully giving each care to the Lord. She tore out the page and ripped it into tiny pieces before throwing it in the trash—a symbol of letting it go and giving it to Him. She returned to her bedroom, ready to experience God's peace and rest.

God, You know every worry I have.
You know me and those things that concern me.
Teach me how to give those things to You
so that I can truly know Your peace.

Listen Closely

Likewise the Spirit helps us in our weakness. For we do not know what to pray for as we ought, but the Spirit himself intercedes for us with groanings too deep for words.

ROMANS 8:26 ESV

When children begin to speak their first words, parents listen closely. But as they grow, the busyness of life can crowd in and parents miss the words their children say. Children want to be heard—even when they're not so little.

The gift of listening promotes healthy relationships with your children, and with your heavenly Father. Give the gift of listening—and really take the time to focus on the one who is sharing their heart and their life. Just listen.

Spend time with God, ask Him to help you learn to listen. As you go throughout your day, He is speaking. He will show you keys to hearing what your children are saying as you tune in to Him. As you really listen, you'll receive insight into your child's life. Don't allow yourself to be distracted but really focus your heart and mind on God and your children.

Lord, help me to hear You and to encourage my children today with active listening. I want to make the time to hear their hearts and give them the precious gift of my undivided attention.

Just You and God

But when you pray, go into your [most] private room, and,
closing the door, pray to your Father, Who is in secret; and
your Father, Who sees in secret, will reward you in the open.

MATTHEW 6:6 AMP

Perhaps when you were a child, you had a secret hideout
or a private place where you would go that was special to
you. Maybe it was a tree house your grandfather built, a
place in the woods where the creek flowed, or even a field
where the corn grew tall and you felt safe from the big
world.

Spiritually, God wants to have a secret place where
the two of you share quiet moments. In your secret place,
you can shut out the voices of the day and discover how

little everything else matters, but God. He holds the whole world in His hands. He can turn the hearts of kings. Whatever you have need of—He can deliver it.

No one knows the path He's chosen for you. In those still moments with Him, He draws you a map and points you toward the truth. Only He brings about the results He destined for you before the beginning of time.

God, You know me best! When I come into my secret place of prayer, it's easy to find You. You are always with me. I open my heart to receive Your love and direction. Teach me Your ways as I choose to spend more time hidden away with You.

Lord, Are We There Yet?

Exclaim over your offerings, celebrate your sacrifices,
give you what your heart desires, accomplish your plans.
When you win, we plan to raise the roof and lead the
parade with our banners. May all your wishes come true!

PSALM 20:3–5 MSG

Sometimes family road trips can make you want to skip the journey altogether, but you travel the road because you have the destination in mind. A four- to eight-hour road trip with teenagers complaining and fighting in the backseat can make you wonder why you ever thought the trip was a good idea in the first place.

Often your journey to the next breakthrough in your spiritual walk can make you ask, "Dear Lord, are we there yet?" But every disappointment, every misstep, and every mountain you go around for the second or third time brings you closer to the place God has for you.

You may whine, cry, or complain about the person sitting next to you on your trip. Then you realize as the Lord takes you down the road He has set before you, it's best if you just lean back, relax, and experience the joy of His faithful navigation.

Lord, help me to appreciate my journey. Help me not to focus so much on getting there, but instead help me to take it a day at a time. Remind me to celebrate each mile along the way.

Your Substitute

*So we do not lose heart. Though our
outer nature is wasting away, our inner
nature is being renewed day by day.*

2 CORINTHIANS 4:16 ESV

A murderer named Barabbas sat in prison awaiting
his sentence of death when Jesus was brought before
Pilate. Many of the Jewish leaders wanted to get rid of
Jesus because He challenged their faith traditions. Jesus'
ministry gave life and liberty to all who would accept it.
He performed miracles of healing: the lame walked and
the dead came back to life in response to His teaching
and faith. He was tried six times by Jewish and Roman
authorities, but never convicted of a crime that would
bring about the penalty of death.

Barabbas was part of a rebellion against the Roman government. While he might have been a hero among the Jews who hated their Roman ruler, he stood convicted of the very things Jesus was accused of doing.

The crowd that day requested this sinful man, Barabbas, go free and that a sinless man, Jesus, be put to death. It is a picture of the greatest substitution. Barabbas was really scheduled to hang on the cross between the other two thieves, but Jesus took his place. That day He was Barabbas's substitute along with all who have ever sinned.

Jesus, thank You for becoming my substitute. Thank You for bearing my sin and the sins of the world, so that I could know God and have eternal life. You are truly my Lord and Savior.

Not Just Another To-Do

"Watch and pray, lest you enter into temptation.
The spirit indeed is willing, but the flesh is weak."
MATTHEW 26:41 NKJV

Have you ever felt like your quiet time with God was just one of the many things on your to-do list? Life is busy with work, school, home, family, friends, and commitments. It's easy to fill your schedule with more than you can really accomplish. It's easy to look up after several days of too much to do and realize that your time with Him isn't what you really want it to be.

Stop! Take a breath and recover. Examine your life and find those things that are less important to get done. Take them off the list. Then kick back, relax, and fellowship with the One who knows you better than you know yourself. Time with Him should refresh and renew you. It shouldn't stress you out.

Father God, forgive me for letting time get away from me.
I don't want to neglect my time with You. I need You.
You are my life and my strength. Show me what things
are most important for my to-do list. Give me strength
to balance my life according to Your desires.

He Came for the Brokenhearted

Search for them as you would for silver; seek them like
hidden treasures. Then you will understand what it means
to fear the Lord, and you will gain knowledge of God.
PROVERBS 2:4–5 NLT

When faced with disappointment and sorrow, you may
be tempted to isolate yourself. The enemy will encourage
you to invite him to a private pity party. Shame, unbelief,
doubt, self-pity, and ugly self-talk are just a few of the
friends he invites to join your party.

In moments your circumstances seem more than you
can bear, instead of a pity party—cry out to God. He came
to heal the brokenhearted (Isaiah 61). The quiet moments
in which you share your hurts with Him can bring peace
and healing. As you open your heart to Him and present it
bare and vulnerable, He can repair it and make it new.

Sometimes the pain is so much that it makes God feel far away. It's okay. He is there. He knows the pain, the hurt you feel. He knows your thoughts and what you need.

Heavenly Father, I am hurting. Instead of isolating myself, I invite You to come in and heal my broken heart. Fill me with Your peace and strength. Thank You for always being there.

From Stressed to Blessed

I press on toward the goal to win the
[supreme and heavenly] prize to which
God in Christ Jesus is calling us upward.

PHILIPPIANS 3:14 AMP

Does it ever seem as if your life is moving across life's movie screen on fast-forward? It's easy to look up and realize you've chosen an overcommitted, stressed-out, and overwhelmed life. It hurts to discover that someone you made a promise to will experience disappointment because you failed to deliver instead of refusing to make the commitment in the first place.

Perhaps you have difficulty telling others "no" when they ask for your help. Maybe you need a better understanding of how to manage your time so that you can accomplish the tasks and keep the commitments you've made.

Taking a quiet moment to hit the Pause button and share some quiet time with God allows you to be more realistic about what you can accomplish in a day. That time in prayer and reflection can provide godly wisdom and discernment about what commitments He wants you to make. The Holy Spirit is here to help you keep your promises.

Lord, forgive me for allowing myself to become overcommitted. I know it is not Your will for me to feel stressed and overwhelmed. Give me wisdom to manage my time and energy.

Living from the Inside Out

> *But if the Spirit of Him who raised Jesus from the*
> *dead dwells in you, He who raised Christ from*
> *the dead will also give life to your mortal bodies*
> *through His Spirit who dwells in you.*
>
> ROMANS 8:11 NKJV

When Adam and Eve sinned, they were turned inside out, much like a T-shirt. Everything once on the inside came out, and what was on the outside turned in. The change may have been gradual or immediate. But they became much more aware of the physical, and less mindful of the spiritual areas of their lives.

Adam and Eve experienced spiritual death. Sin severed their connection with the Spirit. Where their spiritual senses had been dominant, their physical senses became their source of information about their world outside the Garden. All people after them became less and less responsive to their spiritual senses, turned wrong side out as a result of the fall.

That is why you need Jesus. He is the doorway to the Spirit-led life. Through love, God allowed Jesus to trade His righteousness for your sin and provided an opportunity for you to walk and talk with God. When you accept Christ, the Holy Spirit begins a transformation— your spiritual senses come alive and you can hear, touch, taste, smell, and see the things of God as much as Adam and Eve did in the Garden of Eden. You have been restored to God fully.

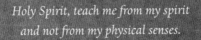

*Holy Spirit, teach me from my spirit
and not from my physical senses.*

We must focus on prayer as the main thrust to accomplish God's will and purpose on earth. The forces against us have never been greater, and this is the only way we can release God's power to become victorious.

JOHN MAXWELL

Trust

Trust Your Accountability Partner

By his divine power, God has given us everything we
need for living a godly life. We have received all of this
by coming to know him, the one who called us to himself
by means of his marvelous glory and excellence.

2 PETER 1:3 NLT

As the project manager for her company, Dena was tired
of continued broken promises made by a coworker to
meet his deadlines. Repeatedly he would commit to a
deadline, only to miss it again and again.

She walked into his office and closed the door.
"What's wrong?" he asked.

"I don't trust you anymore," she answered. "You make
promises to meet your deadlines and you continue to let

your team down. You don't keep your word—and now I don't trust you to do what you say."

He was obviously hurt. "I never thought of deadlines as a trust issue," he said. "Honestly, I've never had someone hold me accountable. I'm sorry. From now on, I'll keep the commitments and meet my deadlines." That day Dena's coworker also became her friend. He appreciated her taking the time to express her concern and hold him accountable.

The Holy Spirit wants to be your accountability partner, but He needs an invitation from you.

Holy Spirit, I invite You to become my accountability partner. I ask You to convict me and confront me on the matters of my heart. I trust You to show me how I can be all that God created me to be!

You Have a Hero

*But as for me, I will look to the Lord and confident in Him
I will keep watch; I will wait with hope and expectancy
for the God of my salvation; my God will hear me. Rejoice
not against me, O my enemy! When I fall, I shall arise;
when I sit in darkness, the Lord shall be a light to me.*

MICAH 7:7–8 AMP

Do you ever need a hero? Once you invite the Lord into
your life, He becomes a constant companion. There are no
secrets hidden from Him. Even when you try to squeeze
Him out of the picture, He is still there—waiting patiently
for you to realize you need Him. He wants to be there for
you when life is good, and when it's difficult.

Most likely God has rescued you many times over
throughout your life. You may not have even recognized

His intervention. It could be as simple as His prompting to take a different route to work—avoiding a tragic accident. Maybe He comforted you in the midst of an abusive and violent childhood. From the small to the very life-threatening situations in your life, God was always there—reaching out, lifting you up, and pulling you out of whatever mess you were in.

He is your Hero. He is always with you—the truest of all heroes.

God, thank You for being with me every day.
Thank You for being my Hero.

The Finder of All Lost Things

I will seek the lost, and I will bring back the strayed,
and I will bind up the injured, and I will strengthen
the weak, and the fat and the strong I will destroy.
I will feed them in justice.

EZEKIEL 34:16 ESV

Rebecca had lost her mother's wedding ring—a ring given to her on her twenty-first birthday. The ring was very important to her. It represented a time when her parents truly loved each other. Wearing it gave her some comfort in spite of her distant relationship with her absent father. But weeks had passed and it was lost.

"God, You know how important this ring is to me. Send Your angels to recover it and bring it back to me," she prayed. A few hours later while she was vacuuming under the dining table—a place she'd checked and rechecked for the ring—she saw something shiny at the corner of one of the chair legs. It was the ring!

God is faithful to take care of even the smallest detail of your life. Is there something missing in your life? Ask God to help you rediscover it.

God, create a fire in me to know You more. I have holes in my life that only You can fill. You are the One who can restore the gap and reconnect those things that need repair. I trust You to find those lost things for me.

Take a Reflection Break

Jesus said, "Come off by yourselves; let's take a break and get a little rest." For there was constant coming and going. They didn't even have time to eat.

MARK 6:31 MSG

In the three years of Jesus' ministry on the earth, He was busy. He constantly gave of Himself to others in so many ways. He was pouring out His wisdom, knowledge, physical strength, and emotional energy—just as you do as you go through your daily life. In His wisdom, He knew His limits and made time to get away to fill up again and be renewed.

When Jesus took a break, He went to places of solitude and quiet, where He could be alone with His heavenly Father. His examples of quiet moments are shared throughout the Bible to demonstrate how you can connect with God—just as He did during His time on earth.

Make sure you take time to get quiet and get alone with God. Share your heart, reflect on where you've been and where you're going. Ask God if you're walking things out according to His plan and direction for your life. Check with Him about the things you will say and do today. Let Him speak to you and fill you with His strength.

Lord, it's hard for me to be still. Teach me how to be still and be quiet. Remind me of the things You would have me to say and do.

A Bigger Dream

A man's heart plans his way,
*but the L*ORD *directs his steps.*

PROVERBS 16:9 NKJV

❧

A common question adults ask of young children is, "What do you want to be when you grow up?" Children have some big dreams at very tender ages. Responses can be very realistic: a doctor, a fireman, a mommy or daddy; or they can be fictional: a superhero, a frog, or a princess. No matter—the dream, anything, seems possible to children.

That's probably why Jesus encouraged everyone to come to Him as little children. The faith of a child is big. They believe anything can happen. As children become adults, their faith is often challenged and their level of belief seems to diminish as circumstances occur, dreams lie dormant and go unrealized.

The truth of God's Word is clear that He is able to do exceedingly, abundantly above all that we can ask or think (Ephesians 3:20). His power within each believer brings His will to pass. So whatever you can believe—in agreement with His desire for your life—can happen. It's time to dream again. Whatever you can dream—God's plans are greater!

God, revive the dreams I've set aside. Give me insight into Your plans for my life. Show me the way You have prepared for me. Open the doors of opportunity that will bring about Your purpose for my life. I choose to do it Your way today.

Always Accepted–Never Alone

I can never escape from your Spirit! I can never get away
from your presence! If I go up to heaven, you are there;
if I go down to the grave, you are there.

PSALM 139:7–8 NLT

Your heavenly Father loves you with an everlasting love.
There is nothing you can do to make Him stop loving
you. No matter where you've been or what you've done,
He loves you. He knows it all and has seen it all. You may
want to run or hide, but you can never be lost from Him.

Perhaps you've had seasons when people have hurt
you. Those memories may keep you from opening up to
others. You may feel like you need to guard your heart and

not let others see the real you. You don't have to pretend with your heavenly Father. He knows it all and loves you with all your baggage. You can bring it to Him and He'll take care of it. He'll accept you as you are today and never leave you alone. You can trust Him.

Heavenly Father, thank You for loving me. Thank You for the knowledge that I can trust You. I want to relax in Your presence and just be myself. There is nothing You don't know. I can rest in You, knowing I am loved and accepted.

When It Seems Like God Says No

*But I trust in you, O L*ORD*; I say, "You are my God."*
My times are in your hand; rescue me from the hand
of my enemies and from my persecutors!

PSALM 31:14–15 ESV

Why does it seem that sometimes God says no to the things you want or think you need? You want to buy a particular house, and God knows this is a desire of your heart. You want to go to college, but the finances keep coming up short. You pray and believe for someone to be healed, but they continue to struggle with disease.

The Bible promises God is only good, and gives good gifts to His children (Matthew 7:9–10). It is during those times you grow most in your faith as you lean on and trust in Him. When you give your heart to Him, and live fully committed to His ways, you grow toward Him and the desires of your heart come in line with His desires.

What you may perceive as no, can really be a time to wait and see what God will do. In the end, He will do you good!

Father, I am struggling with some things that You have said no to. I trust that You know what is best for me. I choose today to let it go. I leave this with You and believe You will work all things out in the way that is best for me as I surrender to You.

When You're Overwhelmed

I will be glad and rejoice in Your mercy, for You have considered my trouble; You have known my soul in adversities, and have not shut me up into the hand of the enemy; You have set my feet in a wide place.

PSALM 31:7–8 NKJV

❧

Macy's heart was heavy. Her family had suffered much loss this past year—starting with the tragic and unexpected death of her older brother in a drunk-driving incident. Grandpa had gone to heaven shortly thereafter. She had lost a job she loved due to cutbacks, and now it seemed her husband's job was in danger.

She poured herself another cup of coffee and sat down to the classified section from last Sunday's newspaper.

The house was unusually silent. She checked on the baby sleeping and then realized she hadn't turned on any praise music.

Tears formed in her eyes as she finally responded to the tug in her heart. She was angry, hurt, and felt alone. She had pushed God aside. . . . "But enough is enough!" she said aloud. "God, forgive me and help me," she whispered. Relief flooded her heart as her fears escaped. She felt God's strong assurance and comfort surround her. He would help her get through this.

God, sometimes life is overwhelming. I know that You are good and You give good gifts. Help me to see the good gifts in the midst of difficulty. Give me courage to trust You today.

Secure in His Promises

This hope is a strong and trustworthy anchor for our souls.
It leads us through the curtain into God's inner sanctuary.

HEBREWS 6:19 NLT

The Word is truth; it never changes. From the very beginning of time His principles are proven faithful. The lives of those recorded in the Bible reflect pictures of promises kept by the Creator. You can count on God to make good on every promise He's ever made.

Some choose to focus on God's Word as a book of commands to follow, as if He wanted to control and command lives. When His children discover relationship with the Father, they can truly know Him and realize His Word contains promise after promise that He will never break.

Taking a step past religion into relationship, those who know Him discover His truths will comfort and revive them. His Word offers security and hope. His faithfulness is something to hold fast to and to depend on no matter what storms challenge their faith. Rather than chains that confine, His powerful Word offers light in a dark world, points out danger, and leads believers to safety.

God, revive my soul with Your wise counsel. My love for Your promises keeps my footsteps steady and safe. Help me to realize my mistakes and forgive my faults. Let my words and thoughts be pleasing to You. You steady me with Your Word.

For each new morning with its light,
For rest and shelter of the night,
For health and food, for love and friends,
For everything Thy goodness sends.
RALPH WALDO EMERSON

Love Came for You

I will confess, praise, and give thanks to You,
for You have heard and answered me;
and You have become my Salvation and Deliverer.

PSALM 118:21 AMP

Some look for love in relationships with others—finding the right husband, having a child to love, or a group of friends who are trusted to always be there. But there is a love that came just for you. No matter who you are, where you've been, or what you think you have done—because of God's great love for you—Jesus came for you.

There is no greater love and no person willing to sacrifice more than your heavenly Father did when He sent

Jesus to earth for you. Love offered an exchange: His life for yours, His purity for your sin, His obedience for your unwillingness.

His love carries the power and grace you need for any challenge you're facing—any circumstance that life has thrown at you. His love is more than enough for you. He paid the price, broke through the shame, counted the cost, and determined you are worthy of His love. Wherever you are today—His love will meet you there.

Heavenly Father, thank You for loving me!
Thank You for counting me worthy of
Your love. I am grateful that You willingly
sent Love to earth for me.

You Can, Because He Can!

Pray diligently. Stay alert,
with your eyes wide open in gratitude.

COLOSSIANS 4:2 MSG

❧

It's normal to want to be independent, self-sufficient.
You see that independent spirit early in children—from a
toddler who wants to do it herself, to a teen who doesn't
want Mom and Dad's advice. It can go against human
nature to have to depend on others for the things we want
and need. Yet, there are times when help from others is
necessary. The Creator of the universe intended for people
to need one another, to rely on community and family. He
also created humankind to be dependent on Him.

Faith in action is believing you can because He can. The connection to God is vital to your success in the simple day-to-day, as well as the big, daunting challenges you face. What challenge are you facing? God is able to turn things right side up for you. Remain thankful for His influence, provision, and direction. Take time out to pray and seek His plans. Then follow through with faith in action. Know you can, because He can. Remain thankful and grateful through the trial knowing He'll bring you out!

Heavenly Father, thank You for Your faithfulness to deliver me! Help me to hold fast to the truth and trust You. I know You will travel this difficult journey with me. I will follow You through it, believe You, and come out triumphant. I know I can, because You can through me!

That Place Only Joy Can Fill

Rejoice in hope, be patient in tribulation,
be constant in prayer.
ROMANS 12:12 ESV

You've met those people—the ones who are just happy all the time, filled with a deep well of joy that seems to bubble over continuously. It may surprise you if you looked behind the scenes of their lives and discovered the pain, the hurt, the challenges in life that they have overcome, and perhaps still struggle with.

Think of that woman who constantly speaks encouraging words to everyone. She makes you feel as if you're the only one she sees when you walk into a room. Surprisingly, she has a daughter in prison, whom she raised in church. Her daughter chose to go away from the things of God. She battles pain and fatigue as leukemia has come back a second and third time, threatening her life. Unknown to anyone, her husband has created a terrible financial mess—and yet she overflows with joy, never complaining.

She has made a decision to be content. She shares her difficulties in those quiet moments with only one audience—her Lord! She chooses joy and He fills the hole in her heart with His love, His presence. She has found her place of peace.

Lord, fill me with a joy that never runs dry. I am thirsty for Your presence. Allow my quiet moments with You to overtake my hurts and overflow with a joy that can only come from You.

Peace Be Still

Oh, give thanks to the LORD, for He is good!
For His mercy endures forever.

1 CHRONICLES 16:34 NKJV

Impatience can cause a reaction—often in anger. When impatience is allowed to push your buttons, the results can leave your heart hurt and discouraged by the emotional charge. James tells us to "count it all joy when you fall into various trials, knowing that the testing of your faith produces patience. But let patience have its perfect work, that you may be perfect and complete, lacking nothing. If any of you lacks wisdom, let him ask of God, who gives to all liberally and without reproach, and it will be given to him. But let him ask in faith, with no doubting" (James 1:2–6 NKJV).

When you are still, patiently waiting for direction from God, you are more composed. Patience allows action to come from the Spirit instead of through emotions. If you can sit on the emotions for a moment or two, it gives your spirit time to align with God's Spirit, so you'll respond in a Christlike way. God is called the God of patience and consolation in Romans 15:5. God desires for His own virtue and character to be reflected in His children. Patience is one reason love never fails.

Lord, teach me to wait on You. When I want to react, help me to control my emotions and give my spirit time to respond the way You desire.

Second Chances

*"But I will offer sacrifices to you with songs
of praise, and I will fulfill all my vows.
For my salvation comes from the Lord alone."*

JONAH 2:9 NLT

Poor Jonah. He wanted to do things his way—not God's.
He didn't want to go and preach to the people of Nineveh.
He had other plans, and he disobeyed God and took his
own path, which eventually found him in the belly of a
huge fish. When he finally realized that his way wasn't
working out as well as he planned, he cried out to God to
save him.

It's easy to convince yourself, like Jonah did, that you
have the better plan. Maybe you've thought your way

would save God some time and trouble. The truth is, you are never alone. God is always there.

Perhaps you've made some choices that went contrary to God's very best for your life. Don't worry, God won't let you miss out on the blessings He has for you. He is only a prayer away. Jonah repented and God made the fish spit him out. Then Jonah realized that God was his salvation. His way was the best way—and he went to Nineveh rejoicing and thanking God for a second chance.

*God, I've blown it. Forgive me. I give
You all my hopes, dreams, and plans.
I lay them at Your feet and will do what
You lead me to do. I choose Your way today.*

Instead, Give Thanks

Yes, let us know (recognize, be acquainted with, and understand) Him; let us be zealous to know the Lord [to appreciate, give heed to, and cherish Him]. His going forth is prepared and certain as the dawn, and He will come to us as the [heavy] rain, as the latter rain that waters the earth.

HOSEA 6:3 AMP

Jana stirred her coffee slowly and looked across the table at her girlfriend Michelle, who had agreed to meet her after Jana had had a bitter fight with her younger brother. "So, why is it that the people I give the most to in life seem to be the least grateful? I am always there for him—emotionally, physically, and financially when he repeatedly screws up. But he treats me like I'm the terrible sister!"

Michelle was gentle. "I'm sure God has felt that way about me. Why do we forget to be thankful—not just to one another, but to the Lord?" Jana leaned in. "Remember how Jesus healed ten lepers, but only one came back to thank Him," Michelle continued.

Jana wanted to be angry with her brother, but Michelle's words convicted her. "You're right," she said. "Instead of whining about my brother's ungracious heart, I need to forgive him and repent for my own ungratefulness."

Father, forgive me for focusing on myself and the hurt I've experienced from others. Instead remind me of Your wonderful goodness. Help me to give You thanks for the many things You are doing right now in my life.

Grateful for All Things Good

Everything God created is good, and to be received with
thanks. Nothing is to be sneered at and thrown out.

1 TIMOTHY 4:4 MSG

God declared everything "good" from the very beginning
of creation, and yet the world is full of pain, suffering,
greed, and waste. Much of humankind has taken God's
good gifts to be used and abused for their own selfish gain.

 Many wonder how God could allow such horror,
but the truth is, God gave the world to humankind. The
human race submitted that dominion and authority to
God's enemy, Satan. Through Satan's influence those
things God created for good have been used for things God
never intended.

It's time to take back the gifts God has given, give thanks to Him for them, and use them for good. God gives wisdom, knowledge, and revelation. One example of that is technology. Think of television and the film industry. Some choose to use that technology to produce horror movies, porn, or trashy comedy. Others use it to share the Gospel throughout the world.

God created all things good. His light and life is all around—casting out the shadows of darkness and bringing faith instead of fear.

Heavenly Father, thank You for the good You've placed in my world. When I am challenged with the consequences of living in a fallen world, show me Your light. Help me to see the good that You created for me.

God of the Angel Armies

God is a safe place to hide, ready to help when we need him. We stand fearless at the cliff-edge of doom, courageous in seastorm and earthquake, before the rush and roar of oceans, the tremors that shift mountains. Jacob-wrestling God fights for us, GOD-of-Angel-Armies protects us.

PSALM 46:1–3 MSG

❦

We live in a fallen world full of sin and corruption. The evening news highlights the disasters, destruction, and evil in this world and can bring fear of the reality we live in. Threats of terrorism, hurricanes, and earthquakes could shake our faith if we remain focused on those things, but the psalmist encourages us to believe that the God of the angel armies can shelter you, save you, and protect you as you follow His lead.

God created you, the world you live in, and everything in it that is good. Even if the world were to end, you have no reason to fear. As a child of God, you can have a quiet confidence that He holds your future in His hands. No matter what circumstances surround you, He will take care of you.

God of the angel armies, thank You for Your love and protection. Thank You that You have not given me a spirit of fear, but of power, love, and a sound mind. I can rest, knowing You care for me and hold my future in Your hands.

While Taking the Test

For all things are for your sakes, that grace,
having spread through the many, may cause
thanksgiving to abound to the glory of God.

2 CORINTHIANS 4:15 NKJV

Brandy's ten-year-old son, Marcus, hated math because
it was so difficult for him. Everything else came easy in
school, but test day in his math class stressed him out
to the point that sometimes he would throw up. "It's
something you have to get through," Brandy told him.
"You can do this because the Bible promises you can do *all*
things through Jesus Christ."

Marcus scoffed, "I wish Jesus would take the test for
me." Brandy thought about his words. *Out of the mouth of*

babes. . . How many times had she wished the same thing when she was facing a test of her faith.

She turned her attention back to her son. "Marcus," she said, "if Jesus took the test, then you wouldn't discover the things you need to know to grow in math and in faith. Jesus is with you and He will help you remember the things you studied, but *you* have to take the test. Then, when it's over and you've achieved a passing grade, we can celebrate His faithfulness. He is always there to help us, no matter what test we're taking."

*Lord, thank You for being with me as I
stand in faith, believing Your promises.
When the test is over, I will remember
to give You the glory for my success.*

Coming Home Again

Let us come to him with thanksgiving.
Let us sing psalms of praise to him.

❧

Madison loved coming home to see her parents and was so thankful that her husband's job allowed them to live within a day's driving distance for a trip home. As she drove the miles with her two toddlers sleeping safely in the backseat, she anticipated their arrival.

An hour later, she turned the car into her parents' driveway, turned off the praise music on the radio, and gently woke the kids with the words, "We are at Gammy and Gramps's house!" Madison took the children out of their car seats as her parents came outside to greet them.

Squeals of delight and shouts of excitement erupted from her children as they raced into their grandparents' arms.

Madison stood back, watching for just a few seconds. Suddenly she realized why this part of the journey thrilled her so much. As she watched her children interact with her parents, she thought to herself, *This must be what it's like for God when we come into His presence as His children to spend time with Him.*

Heavenly Father, help me to remember the excitement and thrill of coming to You just as a child comes into the arms of a loving parent or grandparent. You love me so much, and I am excited to spend time with You. Let me experience the thrill of being at home with You again and again.

Announcing the kingdom of God
pushes away the kingdom of darkness.
DARLENE ZSCHECH

Time to Recharge

A time will come, however, indeed it is already here,
when the true (genuine) worshipers will worship the
Father in spirit and in truth (reality); for the Father is
seeking just such people as these as His worshipers.

JOHN 4:23 AMP

Have you ever gotten behind the wheel of your car, turned the key, and discovered the battery was dead? It is the worst sound at often the most inopportune moment. That battery was out of juice—no energy, no get-up-and-go. Most likely you had to recharge the battery with jumper cables in order to get the car started.

Our spirit often responds in the same way when we are disconnected from the energy source of the heart.

God's presence is vital to survival. Much like those jumper cables for the car battery, praise touches the body and worship ministers to the emotions.

Day-to-day experiences in life can drain our spiritual batteries. It's very important to take time to recharge by spending quiet moments in God's presence, with His Word, in prayer, and in worship. Get alone with God each day to recharge.

Father, forgive me for letting the busyness of life take away from my time with You. Help me to establish healthy spiritual habits by staying committed to my quiet moments with You.

His Instrument of Praise

Thank you! Everything in me says "Thank you!"
Angels listen as I sing my thanks. I kneel in worship
facing your holy temple and say it again: "Thank you!"
PSALM 138:1–2 MSG

If you walk into a music store, you'll find a plethora of instruments. Gorgeous guitars, baby grand pianos, harmonicas, violins, and flutes—and all have the potential to bring about a harmonious sound of praise. In all of their beauty, elegance, and masterful design for sound, those instruments are nothing without someone to play them. They will never achieve their purpose without the worshiper.

You were created for worship! Worship comes from the heart and you were fashioned to be the tabernacle of praise. One of the greatest gifts you can give God—aside from your heart through salvation—is worship. You are His instrument of praise!

Lord, I was created to worship You. Teach me how to worship and honor You with my attitude, my words, my song—my life. Remind me to take time to fully express my love and adoration to You for who You are and who You created me to be. Show me how to become Your instrument of praise each day.

Like a Child

For a day in your courts is better than a thousand elsewhere. I would rather be a doorkeeper in the house of my God than dwell in the tents of wickedness.

PSALM 84:10 ESV

Jason had the privilege to accompany the church's mission team to India as the ministry photographer. One night he saw a little girl about six years old in a red dress. She was completely lost in worship. Through the lens of his camera he saw something different. His photographs captured the moment in which her heart was saying, "This is what I was created for."

Back home reviewing his photos, he realized worship isn't taught, but an event that happens within each person as they open up to the presence of their Creator. He looked back on his own life and recognized that as he had grown up, he'd stopped experiencing the faith-filled, childlike worship. He began to recall the many times when God had met him personally in the midst of a time of praise.

At that moment he knelt and asked God to help him to remember what that was like. Then he purposed he would come to God as a child again each time he entered into worship.

God, help me to have childlike faith.
Show me how to come to You with
expectation, as a small child would come
into Your presence. I want to experience You.

Overflowing with Joy

Is anyone among you suffering? Let him pray.
Is anyone cheerful? Let him sing psalms.

JAMES 5:13 NKJV

❦

Monica's joy was obvious, and she carried it with her into her workplace. She couldn't help but hum or sing as she worked in her office. Most of her coworkers seemed fine with her bubbly personality, but it seemed to irritate her boss.

She was very courteous and professional. She was a hard worker and was willing to go the extra mile to help others. On difficult days, she easily lightened the mood and was quick to offer a positive side to things when others in the office were pessimistic.

One afternoon he commented to her gruffly as she brought some papers in to sign, "Do you have to sing all the time?" "No, I don't," she said calmly. "I guess I could try to gripe and complain all the time, but that might be hard for me since I do enjoy my job. I do try to keep it professional, especially when clients are in the office."

Her boss leaned back in his chair and smiled. "I guess I'd rather have happy employees than difficult ones."

Lord, fill me up with Your joy today.
Let praise be continually in my mouth.

He Has Taken Care of It

He brought them into his house and set a meal
before them, and he and his entire household
rejoiced because they all believed in God.

ACTS 16:34 NLT

Elizabeth sat in church with a heavy heart. She had raised
her children in church and now both of them refused
to attend. It wasn't that they had denied God, but their
life choices didn't demonstrate a close relationship with
the Lord. Her oldest daughter had gone away to school
and incurred large school-loan debt against her parents'
counsel. Now, her youngest daughter was in a serious
relationship with a young man who didn't know the Lord.

Her husband looked at her and smiled as the preacher began his message. Elizabeth leaned back and shut her eyes, praying silently, *God, what about my girls?* Deep in her soul she heard an assuring reply. *"Elizabeth, I've already taken care of both of them."* She opened her eyes and sat up quickly, half-expecting someone else to have heard what she heard in her heart. She smiled and thought, *Okay, God. I get it. I'll trust You in my heart until it becomes a reality in my daughters' lives.*

God, I want to trust You with the people I love. Today I take a step of faith and believe You are working in their lives. I trust that You are working in their hearts so they will come to know and love You as I do.

At Home in You

May Christ through your faith [actually] dwell (settle down, abide, make His permanent home) in your hearts! May you be rooted deep in love and founded securely on love, that you may have the power and be strong to apprehend and grasp with all the saints [God's devoted people, the experience of that love] what is the breadth and length and height and depth [of it].

EPHESIANS 3:17–18 AMP

When friends or family visit, you can do everything to help them feel "at home." You may prepare for their arrival by cleaning, providing fresh linens, and planning meals you know they will enjoy.

The Holy Spirit makes His home. He is more than a guest—more like a special resident. Just as you prepare for a guest, it is important to express thanks for His presence in your heart. You can welcome Him each day by spending time alone with Him in prayer, reading your Bible, and offering praise and worship.

Your worship gives Him first priority in your life and gives you opportunities to hear from Him each day. He'll give you direction and specific instruction for your life and family. Your quiet moments each day can make the Holy Spirit feel at home in your heart every day.

Heavenly Father, thank You for the Holy Spirit.
He is my Counselor, Teacher, and Guide. Help me to
give Him first priority in my quiet moments every day.